Curiosi

of

South Wales

A Regional Guide
to the Unusual

by

Edward Gill

S.B. Publications

CONTENTS

	Page
Acknowledgements and Bibliography	vi
Introduction	vii-viii

CHEPSTOW:

German Submarine Gun	1
Old Father Time	2
A Regicide's Gaol	3

TINTERN:

The Old Railway Station	4

MONMOUTH:

Famous Sons of Monmouth	5
Remember John Renie	6
A Gateway to Wales	7
The Naval Temple and the Round House	8

RAGLAN:

A Castle fit for the King	10

LLANFIHANGEL CRUCORNEY:

The Oldest Inn in Wales	11

CAPEL-Y-FFYN:

St. Mary's Chapel of Ease	12
Eccentric's Retreat	13

CWMYOY:

The Leaning Church	15

CRICKHOWELL:

Little Church in the Hills	16

ABERGAVENNY:

An Olympic Champion's Grave	18

BLAENAVON:

Big Pit — The Old Coal face of Wales	19

NANTYGLO:

Fortified Round Towers	20

EBBW VALE:

Memorial to a Welsh Wizard	21

TREDEGAR:
A Clock in honour of Wellington 22

CAERLEON:
A Roman Theatre 23
The Riverside Inn where Tennyson mused 24

NEWPORT:
A Palace in Wales 25
Grave of Sir Briggs 26
The Cefn Mabli Shovelboard 27
The Transporter Bridge 28

CAERPHILLY:
A Castle with a Leaning Tower 29

CARDIFF:
A Romantic Extravaganza 30
Lord Tredegar's Statue 32
Gareth Edwards' Statue 33
The Pierhead Building 34
Captain Scott's Memorial Lighthouse 35
Welsh Folk Museum 36

TONGWYNLAIS:
Castell Coch — A "Medieval" Extravaganza 41

PONTYPRIDD:
Welsh National Anthem Memorial 43
Old Stone Bridge 44

LLANTRISANT:
Pioneer of Cremation 45

PENARTH:
Old Custom House 46

LAVERNOCK POINT
Marconi Memorial 47

ST. NICHOLAS:
Prehistoric Burial Chambers 48

COWBRIDGE:
Coffin Stile 49

ST. DONAT'S:
Millionaire's Castle 50

NEWTON NOTTAGE:
Pre-Reformation Stone Wall Pulpit 51

MARGAM:
Margam Abbey Orangery 52

PORT TALBOT:
Grave of Dic Penderyn 53

ABERCRAVE:
Castle Home of the Queen of Song 54

SWANSEA:
British Empire Panels 56

OYSTERMOUTH/MUMBLES:
Mumbles Railway Windows 58
Bowdler's Grave 59
Santiago Bells 60
Mumbles Lighthouse 61

GOWER:
Pigeon Cote & Granary 62
Memorial to Lifeboatmen 63
Memorial to an Antarctic Hero 64

BUILTH WELLS:
Memorial to Prince Llywelyn 65

LLANDOVERY:
Mailcoach Memorial 66

LLANARTHNEY:
Paxton's Tower 67

LAUGHARNE:
Dylan Thomas' Boat House 68
Dylan Thomas' Grave 69

CAREW:
Carew Castle 70
Celtic Cross 71

FISHGUARD:
Last Invasion of Britain 72

CWM-YR-EGLWYS:
St. Brynach's Chapel 74

NEVERN:
Celtic Cross 75
Pentre Ifan Cromlech 76

ST. DAVIDS:
St. Non's Chapel and Holy Well 77
Relic of a Saint 79

MILFORD HAVEN:
Nelson Hotel 80

PEMBROKE DOCK:
Early Postal Vending Machine 81

PEMBROKE
Pembroke Castle 82

ANGLE:
Fishermen's Chapel, Dovecote and Pele Tower 83

BOSHERTON:
St. Govan's Chapel 85

TENBY:
Tudor Merchant's House 86
Memorial to a Mathematical Genius 87
Cadavar Tomb of Thomas Danby 87
Gothic Lime Kilns 88

Front Cover: The Ages of Man, Fireplace, Castell Coch, Tongwynlais.
Back Cover; Last Invasion of Britain plaque, Royal Oak Inn, Fishguard.

ACKNOWLEDGEMENTS

I am indebted to the Wales Tourist Board for permission to use their photographs, and particularly Miss Sian Norton of their Cardiff Office. My thanks are also due to: Mr. Roger Worsley for allowing me to use his photographs of the Cadaver Tomb and the Lime Kilns, Tenby; Mr. David Freeman and the Newport Borough Council for the photograph of the Cefn Mabli Shovelboard; and to the many anonymous authors of Church Guides for their invaluable notes. Finally I must acknowledge the National Trust and CADW for their invaluable work in preserving our heritage for our own and future generations.

BIBLIOGRAPHY

Barber, Chris (Ed): *Hando's Gwent.*

Brinn, David: *Adelina Patti.*

Brinton, Piet & Worsley, Roger: *Open Secrets — Exploration in South Wales..*

Denning, Roy: *Story of St. Donat's Castle.*

Edmunds, George: *The Gower Coast.*

Egan, David: *People, Protest and Politics.*

Freeman, David: *Tredegar House.*

Freeman, E. C. & Gill, Edward: *Nelson and the Hamiltons in Wales and Monmouthshire.*

Freeman, Eric: *A Recorde of Tenby.*

Gill, Edward: *Nelson and the Hamiltons on tour.*

Hilling, J. B.: *Shire County Guide to Glamorgan.*

Johnson, Anthony M.: *Scott of the Antarctic and Cardiff.*

Kinross, John: *Fishguard Fiasco.*

Kissack, Keith: *Victorian Monmouth.*

Kissack, Keith: *Monmouth and its buildings.*

Lewis-Thomas, Norman: *Mumbles Past and Present.*

Moorhead, Alan: *Gallipoli.*

Plommer, William (Ed): *Kilvert's Diary.*

Rousham, Sally: *Castell Coch.*

Scandrett, W: *Old Tredegar.*

Thomas, Ruth: *South Wales.*

Thorne, Roy: *History of Penarth.*

Vaughan-Thomas, Wynford: *New Shell Guide to South and Mid-Wales.*

Williams, Stuart: *Vale of History.*

Williams, Herbert: *Stage coaches in Wales.*

Woolley, Hilary: *Sir Frank Brangwyn — Studies for the British Empire Panels.*

INTRODUCTION

I first came to South Wales from Lancashire over thirty-five years ago. My entry into the Principality was made by a perilous ferry crossing of the River Severn from Aust to Beachley. In those far off days before motorways or the Severn Bridge, road travel, even for short distances, could be even more tortuous than it is today. The very mention of South Wales conjured up in the minds of most people, and certainly in mine, grim mining valleys and steel works belching great clouds of smoke. The once beautiful landscape was scarred by ugly black mountains of spoil, and all too frequently the very life of mining communities was imperilled by the overshadowing tip as it was at Aberfan. On landing at Beachley, I drove through the Wye Valley to Monmouth, and was spellbound by its beauty. There were lots of surprises ahead, from Chepstow in the east to Milford Haven in the west. Almost immediately, my perception of South Wales started to change.

Since then, nearly all the mines have been closed, and steel works such as Ebbw Vale, have given way to new and cleaner industries. New roads have opened up the valleys, and the ugly mountainous tips have been transformed into gentle green slopes on which sheep now graze.

The people of South Wales are taking a new look at their environment and rediscovering many objects of interest that hitherto have been ignored or simply taken for granted. Examples of these are Newport's elegant Tredegar House, which contrasts sharply with the grey stone round Towers a few miles distant at Nantyglo. Yet each are curious objects of interest, and take their place as part of the historical heritage. Some objects are less obvious and perhaps more obscure. Travellers through Wales are often in such a hurry to get to their destinations, that they miss much of the interest along the way. How many motorists speeding to west Wales along the A40, have noticed the curious stone obelisk on the roadside two miles east of Llandovery? How many have asked themselves why it is there, and how many have stopped to find out the answer?

Visitors from all over the world are coming to Wales in ever increasing numbers. They are attracted by its natural beauty, and by many objects of interest and curiosity, from the leaning tower at Caerphilly Castle, to John Renie's gravestone in Monmouth churchyard.

The word 'curiosities' is used in its broadest sense to describe objects that are of unusual, architectural, or historical interest. Access to many of the objects is free and unrestricted, others are privately owned, and you are requested to respect their privacy. Access is sometimes restricted, particularly where CADW or the National Trust are in charge of the property, and I have endeavoured to indicate where this is so. This book is by no means a definitive guide to all curiosities in the area. However, it provides a wide selection for visitors and local residents alike. I hope this book will give you as much pleasure in searching out its curious objects, as I have had writing about them. It might even prompt the reader to search for other curiosities. If you find any more, please let us know, we could consider a second volume!

THE AUTHOR

Born in Manchester, Edward Gill has lived for most of his life in the country since leaving the city for Shropshire as a wartime evacuee. Much of the past thirty-five years has been spent in South Wales, where he developed a particular interest in Monmouth, about which he has written and broadcast. In 1987, his book, *Nelson and the Hamiltons on Tour* was published. In the book he relates the story of Nelson's triumphant tour in the summer of 1802, from the home he shared with the Hamiltons in Surrey, via Oxford and the Cotswolds through South Wales and the Midlands. The author has motored more than 1½ million miles in the course of his business, and has used the opportunity to explore the places to which he has travelled.

CHEPSTOW, GWENT
GERMAN SUBMARINE GUN

Location: Beaufort Square, Chepstow.

A German submarine gun in the centre of Chepstow might seem rather incongruous, but it has a special significance. It was presented to the town by King George V in recognition of the gallentry of a young Able Seaman from Chepstow, at Gallipoli on the 25th April 1915.

The troopship *River Clyde,* with 2000 men on board, ran aground below Seddul Bahir and was seperated from the shore by a narrow strip of water. Her Captain, Commander Unwin, dived into the sea and swam ashore. Helped by a young Able Seaman called Williams, he lashed some lighters together to form a bridge. Waist deep in water, and under heavy gunfire, both men held on for over an hour until Williams was hit and died of his wounds. Both men were awarded the Victoria Cross.

There is a painting of the scene in Chepstow Church.

CHEPSTOW, GWENT
OLD FATHER TIME

Location: Parish Church.

An interesting curiosity in Chepstow Parish Church is an 18th-century clock mechanism, made by a local clockmaker. On the 7th August 1858, an appeal in verse to the Churchwardens for its resoration appeared in the Chepstow Weekly Advertiser.

When Meredith first placed me here,
Of country clocks I was the peer,
My voice was sweet,
My frame was bright,
My pointers ever right and tight.

It is not recorded whether or not the clock was repaired in 1858, but the chimes were repaired in 1882. In spite of its good mechanical state, it was replaced by electricity in 1966.

CHEPSTOW, GWENT
A REGICIDE'S GAOL

> *Location:* Chepstow Castle is in Bridge Street.
> *Access:* Open to the public all year.

Chepstow Castle is rooted in rock high above the waters of the River Wye. It looks impregnable, and no doubt it was when the Normans built it. In the Civil War it was garrisoned for the King, but finally surrendered to Cromwell. After the restoration, the Royalists had their revenge when Henry Marten, a member of the High Court of Justice and a signatory of the King's death warrant, was put on trial. Although his life was spared, he was sentenced to life imprisonment. For over twenty years his gaol was the round tower, now known as Marten's Tower, to the left of the Castle gatehouse. He is buried in the Parish Church under a stone which bears his own epitaph:

> *"My time was spent in serving you and you,*
> *And death's the pay, it seems and welcome too."*

(Wales Tourist Board)

TINTERN
THE OLD RAILWAY STATION

Location: ½ mile north of Tinern on the A466 — signposted.
Access: (Owned by Gwent CC). Open all year.

The railway line from Chepstow to Monmouth, was among the most picturesque in Britain. It was opened in 1876, and for ninety years trains steamed a leisurely 50 minute journey through the 14½ miles of breathtaking scenery along the banks of the Wye.

A curious little relic of those bygone days is Tintern Railway Station. After closing in 1959, it fell into decay and was rescued in 1975 by Gwent County Council. Now restored to its old fashioned self, it is a popular tourist attraction. The refreshment room sells a good cup of tea and excellent home made cakes. Congratulations are due to the County Council for its initiative and the well deserved Civic Trust Award.

MONMOUTH
FAMOUS SONS OF MONMOUTH

Location: Agincourt Square, Monmouth.

Two great sons of Monmouth are commemorated in Agincourt Square. Aviation and motor pioneer Charles Stewart Rolls (born 27 August, 1877), who was killed in an air crash at Bournemouth in 1910, stands on a plinth holding a model of the aircraft in which he died. Unfortunately the tail was damaged when the statue, by no less a sculptor than Goscombe John, was cleaned by sand blasting!

Lift your eyes to a niche in the Shire Hall facade from where a statue of Henry V looks down. The Hero of Agincourt (1415), was born in Monmouth Castle, and though the statue records the date as the 9th August 1387, latter-day historians think it was more likely the 16th September. The statue was erected in 1792, and is the work of Charles Peart of Welsh Newton, who also made busts for Wedgwood.

(Wales Tourist Board)

MONMOUTH
REMEMBER JOHN RENIE

Location: East end of St. Mary's Churchyard, Monmouth.

An amusing and intriguing gravestone is to be found in St. Mary's churchyard at Monmouth. There are fifteen rows of inscription on the stone, each of nineteen letters, making a total of 285. The centre letter is a capital 'H', and whether you read up or down, left to right or even right to left, for row upon row the message is exactly the same — "Here Lies John Renie". It does not say who John Renie was, simply that he died on May 31 in 1832 aged 33 years. Fascinating!

MONMOUTH
A GATEWAY TO WALES

Location: Monnow Street, Monmouth.

The Monnow Gatehouse must be unique in Britain, being the only fortified gateway to survive the passage of time intact, and for its pure architectural beauty. Monnow Bridge was built about 1272. During construction of the flood prevention scheme in 1988, the remains of a much earlier timber bridge, which analysis dates about 1140, were found. The remains have been preserved below the river bed. Monnow Gate has a long and chequered history, having stood astride the bridge for over seven hundred years. In the Civil War it was occupied in turn by Royalists and Roundheads, and in 1839, the tower was prepared for an attack by the Chartists. A much loved landmark in Monmouth, it stands as a Gateway to History.

MONMOUTH
THE NAVAL TEMPLE AND THE ROUND HOUSE

> *Location:* Cross the Wye Bridge and take the A4136 Monmouth to Staunton road for a mile. The Naval Temple is signposted; follow a sharp hairpin turn on the right, and then up the hill on the right.
> *Access:* Both the Naval Temple and Round House are owned by the National Trust. Access is by a good unclassified road to the car park at the top of the Kymin. The Naval Temple is always open.

High on the Kymin Hill overlooking the town of Monmouth is a unique memorial to the British Navy. The Naval Temple was erected 1st August 1800, as a tribute to Britain's great naval admirals who distinguished themselves by their glorious victories for England. In the summer of 1802 the greatest of all those commanders, Lord Nelson, visited the Temple with his beloved Emma, and her husband Sir William Hamilton. The temple is dedicated to Her Grace the Duchess of Beaufort, daughter of Admiral Boscowen.

The celebrated visitors had breakfast in the Round House, which stands just a few feet away, from where they could enjoy the breathtaking panoramic views from east to west, with the Malvern Hills and Brecon Beacons among the most prominent landmarks.

THE FIGURE
WHICH CROWNS THE TEMPLE,
EXHIBITS BRITANNIA, SEATED ON A ROCK:
THE PAINTING IN FRONT, REPRESENTS
THE STANDARD OF GREAT-BRITAIN,
WAVING TRIUMPHANT
OVER THE FALLEN AND CAPTIVE FLAGS OF
FRANCE, SPAIN, AND HOLLAND:
THE OPPOSITE SIDE,
THE GLORIOUS AND EVER-MEMORABLE
BATTLE OF THE NILE.

Plaque on the Naval Temple

The Round House

RAGLAN, GWENT
A CASTLE FIT FOR THE KING

Location: in Raglan on the A40, 7 miles west of Monmouth.

Access: Open all year.

(Wales Tourist Board)

Raglan Castle was built in the 15th century by Sir William ap Thomas on the site of an earlier Norman stronghold. During the Civil War, King Charles I sought refuge at Raglan, after the Battle of Naseby, and played bowls on its lawn. In 1646, the Royalist Marquess of Worcester, then aged 85, held it under seige for nearly three months, against Cromwell's troops, declaring he would rather die nobly than live with infamy. When Fairfax forced its surrender Worcester marched his troops out with flags proudly flying and drums defiantly beating. Encompassed by a moat, it stands today as a beautiful place of peace and tranquility.

LLANFIHANGEL CRUCORNEY, GWENT
THE OLDEST INN IN WALES

Location: The village of Llanfihangel Crucorney is situated on the A465 from Abergavenny to Hereford.

"The Skirrid" is said to be Wales' oldest inn. Set at the foot of the mountain after which it is named, the inn has a long and mysterious past and is reputed to be haunted.

Eight hundred years ago, two brothers were tried at the inn, then called "The Millbrook". Their crime was sheep stealing, for which they were hanged from a beam in the stairwell that was frequently used for the purpose. At least 182 people were executed on the premises having been sentenced by the infamous Judge Jeffries following the unsuccessful Monmouth rebellion.

The Welsh rebel Owain Glyndwr is said to have rallied his troops in the forecourt, and the mounting block used by Glyndwr and many Welsh princes since, still stands outside.

It is now a welcoming inn where visitors can enjoy good ale and good food under its historic roof.

CAPEL-Y-FFYN, GWENT
ST. MARY'S CHAPEL OF EASE

Location: Take the A465 from Abergavenny to Llanvihangel. Crucorney then on unclassified road to Hay-on-Wye.

Capel-y-Ffyn is a remote hamlet in the Black Mountains on what is known as the Gospel Pass. To some it is Kilvert country and to others the place where the sculptor Eric Gill lived an eccentric life in the 1920s.

Lovers of Kilvert will recall how the diarist tramped over eight miles of mountains from Hay on Wye. "... I remember the place perfectly, the old chapel, short stout and boxy with its little bell turret (the whole building reminding me of an owl) the quiet peaceful chapel yard shaded by seven solemn yews". Little has changed — the yews are still there, and so is the chapel. Built in 1762, it replaced an earlier chapel. It has a medieval font, a pulpit of 1780 and five pews, one dated 1783. A lop-sided belfry houses two bells, one medieval, recast in the 19th century. Two gravestones in the churchyard are the work of Eric Gill.

CAPEL-Y-FFYN, GWENT
ECCENTRIC'S RETREAT

Location: Hay-on-Wye road through Llanthony Valley, Gwent.
Access: Open daily, dawn to dusk.

Fifty yards south of the chapel on the opposite side of the road, a lane leads to Llanthony Monastery. Here the Reverend Joseph Leycester Lyne, founded a small monastic community. Known as Father Ignatious, he wore a Benedictine habit, and covered his tonsured head with a cowl. When Kilvert called in 1870, the monks were still constructing the cloisters. "I laid a stone at the particular request of Father Ignatious". The monks have long since left, and the Holy Father lies buried in the ruins of the old church. But peace and an air of mystery remain. Inside the monastery, open to the public, is a tiny Roman Catholic Chapel with a simple altar above which is a Latin text carved by Eric Gill.

Llanthony Monastery

ERIC GILL LIVED AND
WORKED HERE 1924·1928
ALSO HIS ELDEST
DAUGHTER ELIZABETH
ANGELA–BETTY–1924·1956

my work is my leisure · my leisure is my work

Eric Gill Memorial Plaque, Llanthony Monastery

Father Ignatious' grave in the ruins of the old monastery

CWMYOY, GWENT
THE LEANING CHURCH

Location: Take the A465 from Abergavenny to Llanvihangel Crucorney, then the Llanthony road for two miles. Cwmyoy is a mile up a road signposted to the right.

St. Martin's Church, Cwmyoy is shrouded in legend. Its isolation and leaning tower lend it an air of mystery; but it's not just the tower that's odd. No part of this unusual church is square or at right angles with any other part, due to the unstable rock on which it is built.

Set on the pilgrim's route to St. David in Pembrokeshire, the church dates back to the Middle Ages when Christianity was brought to the Black Mountains by St. David himself. Inside is a medieval stone pilgrim's cross, found on a nearby farm in 1871. It was stolen in 1967, and later recovered from a London antique shop.

CRICKHOWELL, POWYS
THE LITTLE CHURCH IN THE HILLS

Location: Take the A465 from Abergavenny to Llanvihangel Crucorney.
Proceed on an unclassified road to Forest Coalpit, then follow signs to Patricio.

The tiny church of Merthyr Issui at Patricio is hidden away in the hills, on a site that predates the Norman Conquest. Tradition says the hermit Issui had a cell near the Holy Well, below where the church now stands. He is said to have been murdered by an ungrateful traveller whom he befriended. The well became a place of pilgrimage. Among the earliest pilgrims was Giraldus Cambrensis, and centuries later the historian Sir Richard Colt Hoare.

Inside the church is a font of 1056, historic wall paintings and a rood loft with an exquisitely carved screen. Few rood lofts survived the reformers zeal, and this is one of Patrico's greatest treasures.

St. Issui's Well, Patricio

St. Issui's Church

Rood loft and carved screen, St. Issui's Church

17

ABERGAVENNY, GWENT
AN OLYMPIC CHAMPION'S GRAVE

Location: Leave Abergavenny through Llanfoist taking the B4246 Blaenavon road, Proceed for two miles before turning left at the signpost for Llanellen. Continue for a mile and park on the Foxhunter car park.

The long and distinguished show jumping career of the great "Foxhunter" culminated in 1952 at the Olympic games in Helsinki. Ridden by Col. Harry Llewelyn, he lead the British team to a Gold Medal. When the old horse died in 1959, his remains were buried on his favourite Blorenge (1833 ft.) where he was regularly exercised. His simple grave among the rocks is marked with a plaque that lists his achievements.

BLAENAVON, GWENT
BIG PIT — THE OLD COAL FACE OF WALES

Location: Leave the A465 Heads of the Valleys road just outside Abergavenny on the B4246 Blaenavon road. Proceed for four miles
following the signs to Big Pit.

Access: Big Pit is owned by Big Pit (Blaenavon) Trust Ltd. It is open to
visitors from 10 am to 3.30 pm daily from March to November.
There is a gift shop as well as good refreshment facilities.

Coal mines in South Wales have closed so quickly over the past 25 years, that they could easily have disappeared leaving little trace of their existence. Fortunately, somebody had the foresight to preserve the Big Pit at Blaenavon as a living museum. Big Pit, or Pwll Mawr as it is known in Welsh, was a working coalmine for over 100 years, until its closure in 1980. It reopened in 1983 as a museum of coalmining where people could experience at first hand, the conditions under which coal-miners worked. From the pithead, visitors can enter the cage used by the miners, to descend 300 ft. down the shaft. A conducted tour takes them along the pit bottom to the workshops, coal face, and the pit ponies' stables. Iron was also mined here, and visitors can see the old ironstone workings. Air doors, operated by children who spent long hours in total darkness underground, are still in place. Above and below ground, Big Pit portrays the grim life of coal mining.

(Wales Tourist Board)

NANTYGLO, GWENT
FORTIFIED ROUND TOWERS

Location: Roundhouse Farm, Nantyglo. Signposted off the A467 Brynmawr to Newbridge road.

Access: The Roundtower complex is privately owned and part of a working farm. Public access is free and there is a small car park. Visitors are requested not to take dogs, and to close all gates.

In the early 19th century, Nantyglo experienced the full force of the industrial revolution. Set in the South Wales coalfields it was ideally situated for the ironmasters Joseph and Crawshay Bailey to exploit its resources. They are also accused of exploiting their workers. Living and working conditions were appalling. Children as young as seven years of age worked long hours in the ironworks.

Simmering unrest and threats of violence prompted the Baileys to build two fortified towers as a refuge for their families. The northern tower pictured here consists of two floors for living accommodation, and a ventilated cellar for the storage of food in case of a seige. A spiral stone staircase set in the four-feet-thick wall, served the living quarters and gave access to the roof. The tower is entered by a solid iron door with two holes for muskets.

The towers are believed to be the last privately-built castle-type fortifications in Britain. They were restored in 1986-1988.

EBBW VALE, GWENT
MEMORIAL TO A WELSH WIZARD

Location: On the Ebbw Vale to Tredegar road.

On a windswept hillside known as Waun-y-Pound between Tredegar and Ebbw Vale, four enormous grey stones stand as a memorial to Aneurin Bevan. One of the most controversial and turbulent political figures of the 20th century, Bevan was member of parliament for the constituency of Ebbw Vale which as the stones record, included Tredegar and Rhymney. Like David Lloyd George before him, Bevan was a wizard with words. During his long parliamentary career, before the days of television electioneering, he frequently addressed mass meetings where the stones now stand. An inscription on one of the stones proclaims: "It was here Aneurin Bevan spoke to the people of his constituency and the world". Bevan died in 1960, and his ashes were scattered at nearby Trefil. The stones were unveiled in the 1970s by Bevan's successor Michael Foot.

TREDEGAR, GWENT
A CLOCK IN HONOUR OF WELLINGTON

Location: Tredegar Town Centre.

An inscription on the clock in the centre of Tredegar records that it was presented to the town from the proceeds of a bazaar. It was the brainchild of Mrs. Mary Elizabeth Davis, who wanted to give the town a present, and decided on a clock. Most of the cost was borne by her husband, with the rest being raised at a bazaar which she organised. Sadly, Mrs. Davis died before its completion in 1858.

The clock was one of the first of a new type made by J. B. Joyce of Whitchurch in Shropshire. It has four faces, and stands on top of a cylindrical cast iron column set in a cast iron plinth. The plinth bears the Royal Arms of England, with a dedication to "Wellington — England's Hero".

CAERLEON, GWENT
A ROMAN THEATRE

Location: The theatre is well signposted.
Access: Open from dawn to dusk.

Caerleon was the Roman Fortress of Isca, where the Second Augusta Legion was based. From here the Roman invaders hoped to surpress the savage Silurian tribes to the west. There is ample evidence of the Roman occupation, but pride of place must go to the Amphitheatre. Built about 80 AD, it was excavated in the 1920s by the distinguished archaeologist Sir Mortimer Wheeler. Looking down on the theatre today, it is not difficult to hear the noise of spectators, and imagine the fun and games that went on there almost two thousand years ago. Dubbed Camelot by Geoffrey of Monmouth, Caerleon has long been linked to the legend of King Arthur.

(Wales Tourist Board)

CAERLEON, GWENT
THE RIVERSIDE INN WHERE TENNYSON MUSED

> *Location:* On the banks of the River Usk, close to the bridge.

On the banks of the Usk at Caerleon is an old country inn called the Hanbury Arms. It has little claim to fame except that in the middle of last century, the great Victorian poet Alfred, Lord Tennyson stayed here. Fascinated by the Arthurian legend, he gazed across the river from a bay window in the Magistrates' Room, and was inspired to pen the lines:

> *The Usk murmurs by the window*
> *As I sit like King Arthur in Caerleon.*

A plaque on the wall commemoraates the inn's association with the poet and his visit during September 1856. It was erected by Monmouthshire Local History Council in September 1956.

NEWPORT, GWENT
A PALACE IN WALES

Location: M4, Junction 28 — then follow the signs from the A48
Access: The House and Gardens are open daily to the public.

Rightly described as a Palace in Wales, Tredegar House is a treasure. Its origins date back to 1402 and among its distinguished visitors was King Charles I. Everything about it is impressive from the ornate Edney Gates (1714), to the oak panelled Dining Room, used by the B.B.C. for the T.V. series "Victorian Kitchen". In the Bell Passage, the long rows of bells are a reminder that an army of servants was only a bell pull away. The Morgans lived here for over 500 years. Best known was Godfrey, 1st Viscount Tredegar who was in the Charge of the Light Brigade at Balacalava. After the last Morgan left in 1951, the house was sold and became a girls school. Having survived that traumatic experience, it was rescued by Newport Borough Council in 1974. Since then it has been carefully restored to its former grandeur and is well worth a visit.

NEWPORT, GWENT
GRAVE OF SIR BRIGGS

Location: Leave the M4 at Junction 28. Follow signs for Tredegar House
Access: The Garden is open daily to the public.

A simple obelisk in the garden of Tredegar House marks the grave of a very distinguished old war horse called Sir Briggs. "Boldly and well" he carried the Hon. Godfrey Morgan, 1st Viscount Tredegar in the Charge of the Light Brigade, with the 17th Lancers, the Death of Glory Boys, at Balacalava in 1854. He also carried his master at the Battles of Alma and Inkerman. His long and eventful life ended in 1874, at the great age of 28 years.

Behind the memorial to Sir Briggs is the grave of Lord Tredegar's favourite Skye Terrier, Peeps.

NEWPORT
THE CEFN MABLI SHOVELBOARD

Location: Tredegar House, Newport.

The Cefn Mabli Shovelboard is a remarkable piece of furniture, being the longest single planked oak table in the world. It was made for Cefn Mabli House, five miles west of Tredegar House.

Thomas Dinely's wrote of it in 1684: "The Gallery of Kevenmably hath in it of note, either fitted to the length thereof, or the Gallery to it, an extraordinary shovelboard of 42 foot in length and of one entire plank of an oak whereof 20 foot was also cut off before!"

The game of shovelboard might best be compared with shove halfpenny. A brass disc was made to slide along the length of the board, and discs that overshot the board were collected in a box or swallowing dish attached to the sides of the table.

NEWPORT, GWENT
THE TRANSPORTER BRIDGE

Location: Stephenson Street, Newport.

In 1898, Newport's Town Bridge provided the only crossing of the River Usk. Widened in 1896, and partly rebuilt in 1892, it was unable to cope with the growing volume of traffic. The cost of erecting a high level bridge that would not impede the passage of shipping was out of the question. A cheaper expedient was the Transporter Bridge, brainchild of Frenchman Monsieur Arondin, and Newport's Borough Engineer, Robert Haynes. It was capable of carrying six vehicles and one hundred foot passengers for 592 feet across the river in a suspended gondola. Lord Tredegar opened the Transporter in 1906, and it continued in use until the opening of George Street Bridge in the 1960s.

CAERPHILLY, MID GLAMORGAN
A CASTLE WITH A LEANING TOWER

Location: Close to the town centre.
Acess: Open daily throughout the year.

Caerphilly can boast the largest castle in Wales, and second only to Windsor in the whole of Great Britain. Unlike most castles that are built on high ground, moated Caerphilly is strategically placed in a hollow, from where it controlled the valleys to the north. It was built by the Marcher Lord Richard de Clare, known as Gilbert 'the Red', between 1268 — 1271 as a defence against Llywelyn ap Gruffudd, the last native Prince of Wales. It is perhaps best known for its precariously leaning tower; a demolition job Cromwell didn't quite complete. Today, the Great Hall is used for feasting and popular 'medieval' banquets.

CARDIFF, SOUTH GLAMORGAN
A ROMANTIC EXTRAVAGANZA

Location: Cardiff city centre.
Acess: Open daily throughout the year.

Cardiff Castle stands on a site that was occupied by the Romans almost 2000 years ago, and traces of their masonry can still be seen in the outer walls. A magnificent Norman keep dominates the castle grounds, but present day visitors will perhaps be more interested in the mock medieval extravaganza inside the Castle. The clock tower (shown on the right of the photograph), built in the romantic style of the middle ages, and embellished on all sides by colourful heraldic shields, and signs of the zodiac, gives a hint of what is inside. The Castle was restored in the latter part of last century by John, 3rd Marquess of Bute and his architect William Burges. Neither effort or expense was spared in creating the colourful ornate interior that makes the castle one of the City's most popular tourist attractions.

Norman Keep and grounds of Cardiff Castle

The fireplace, Library, Cardiff Castle. (The ghost of the Marquiss of Bute is said to pass through the fireplace of the Library, and then through a six-feet-thick wall leading to the Chapel).

CARDIFF, SOUTH GLAMORGAN
LORD TREDEGAR'S STATUE

Location: Cardiff Civic Centre

GODFREY
FIRST · VISCOUNT · TREDEGAR
ERECTED · BY · THE · COUNTY · OF
GLAMORGAN · AS · A · TRIBUTE
OF · RESPECT · AND · AFFECTION

A fine equestrian statue stands in Cardiff's Civic Centre. It is of Godfrey Morgan, 1st Viscount Tredegar mounted on his faithful charger Sir Briggs. Visitors to Tredegar House at Newport, will recall that Sir Briggs was the horse that carried his master in the Charge of The Light Brigade at Balacalava in 1854, and later at the Battles of Alma and Inkerman.

CARDIFF, SOUTH GLAMORGAN
GARETH EDWARDS' STATUE

Location: St. David's Centre, Queen Street, Cardiff.
Acess: The Centre is open during normal shopping hours.

For visitors to Cardiff's bustling St. David's Shopping Centre, memories of the Golden Age of Welsh Rugby are evoked by a bronze statue of Gareth Edwards. One of Wales' greatest players, he is portrayed in a characteristic attacking posture ready to pass the ball. The statue is so lifelike that one is inclined to look for his two celebrated team mates, Phil Bennett and J.P.R. Williams.

CARDIFF, SOUTH GLAMORGAN
THE PIERHEAD BUILDING

Location: West Bute Street.

Like much of South Wales, Cardiff's Docklands is changing beyond recognition, but thankfully, some of its finest buildings have been spared. One is the striking terracotta Pierhead Building overlooking the Bristol Channel. Built in 1897, its style has been described as reminiscent of 16th century French Renaissance. It has an exotic array of hexagonal chimneys, pinaccled turrets and gargoyles. On its west side is an interesting panel depicting a steam locomotive above the coats of arms of the old Cardiff Borough and the Bute family. Beneath is a motto in Welsh "Wrth Ddwr A Than" — By Water And Fire.

CARDIFF, SOUTH GLAMORGAN
CAPTAIN SCOTT'S MEMORIAL LIGHTHOUSE

Location: Roath Park, Cardiff.
Access: The park is open daily to the public.

On the 15th June 1910, Captain Robert Falcon Scott set sail from Cardiff in the S.S. *Terra Nova*, to conquer the South Pole. Before leaving, Scott pledged — "I will reach the South Pole or I will never come back again." The rest is history. In memory of the ill-fated expedition lead by Captain Scott and accompanied by his companions, Captain L. E. G. Oates, Lieutenant H. R. Bowers, Dr. E. A. Wilson and Petty Officer Edgar Evans (see also page 64), a clock tower in the form of a lighthouse was erected at the south end of Roath Park Lake. Surmounted by a model of *Terra Nova,* the tower was erected and presented to the city of Cardiff by F. C. Bowring, J.P. in 1915. The clock tower has since been one of Cardiff's most familiar landmarks.

CARDIFF, SOUTH GLAMORGAN
WELSH FOLK MUSEUM

Location: St. Fagans Village, 4 miles west of Cardiff.
Access: Open to the public daily throughout the year.

The Welsh Folk Museum is a collection of curiosities set in the grounds of St. Fagan's Castle near Cardiff. Since opening in 1946, dismantled buildings have been brought here from all over Wales, to be re-erected and given a new lease of life as examples of Welsh life and culture over many centuries.

There is a beehive pigsty of 1800 from Pontypridd, a 1772 tollhouse from Aberystwyth, and an 18th-century noncomformist chapel that is still used for worship. A magnificent timber framed barn built at Strad Lydan in Clwyd in 1550, was re-erected at St. Fagans in 1951. Welsh sporting life in the 18th century is represented by a cockpit, from the Hawk & Buckle Inn at Denbigh. These living and working farms, cottages, chapels, mills and many other historic buildings have been superbly assembled in a hundred acres of picturesque parkland, all within walking distance. For anyone interested in curiosities, the Welsh Folk Museum is a must.

(Wales Tourist Board)

Workers' Terraced Cottages

Old Thatched Cottage

Toll house, Aberystwyth, c. 1772
(Toll details are shown on the wall on the right)

16th-century thatched barn

Thatched cockpit, Welsh Folk Museum

Interior of cockpit

Beehive pigsty, c. 1800, Welsh Folk Museum

TONGWYNLAIS, MID GLAMORGAN
CASTELL COCH — A "MEDIEVAL" EXTRAVAGANZA

Location: Exit at junction 32 on the M4, 5 miles north of Cardiff. Situated off the A470.

Access: Open daily throughout the year.

The sight of Castell Coch must come as a surprise to anyone travelling on the A470 from Cardiff to Merthyr. Perched on a wooded hillside, the conical roofs of its towers give it the appearance of something out of a fairy tale. It has a drawbridge, courtyard, dungeon and well. But in spite of its medieval appearance, the castle is little more than one hundred years old. It was built in 1891 by John Patrick Crichton Stuart, the romantic 3rd Marquess of Bute, on the site of a 13th-century castle. The romance continues inside, with walls and ceilings extravagantly decorated with colourful painting of scenes from the Bible and Aesops Fables. Lavishly sculptured figures from myth and legend complete the fantasy.

Section of Aesop's Fables wall painting, Castell Coch

The three colourful carved figures above the Drawing Room chimney-piece are from Greek mythology and represent the Three Fates that controlled the destiny of men. Clotho spins the thread of life, as Lachesis measures its length, and Atrepos cuts it at death. The three sit above the Three Ages of Man.

PONTYPRIDD, MID GLAMORGAN
WELSH NATIONAL ANTHEM MEMORIAL

Location: Ynysanghared War Memorial Park.
Access: Park open daily dawn to dusk.

The Welsh National Anthem, 'Hen Wlad Fy Nhadau', was composed by two Pontypridd men. They were father and son, Evan James who wrote the words, and his son James who composed the music. First performed in the Castel Ifor public house at Hopkinstown in 1856, it was an immediate success. In 1930, Pontypridd commemorated this remarkable partnership by erecting an impressive memorial by Sir Goscombe John in Ynysangharad Park, and in 1975, the grave of Evan James was moved to the base of the memorial.

PONTYPRIDD, MID GLAMORGAN
OLD STONE BRIDGE

The old stone bridge across the river Taff at Pontypridd is a truly remarkable structure. It is the work of the Rev. William Edwards, a local minister and self taught mason. In 1750, he was contracted to build a bridge over the Taff for £50. His first attempt was swept away in a flood after only two years, and a second collapsed into the river. Undaunted, he made a third attempt, which is the single arch bridge we see today. It spans 140 feet, is 15 feet wide, and 36 feet high at low water. There are three cylindrical holes on each side of the arch, measuring 9ft, 6ft and 3ft in diameter in ascending order. It had the largest span of any bridge in Britain until London Bridge was built in 1831.

LLANTRISANT, MID GLAMORGAN
PIONEER OF CREMATION

Location: Town Square, Llantrisant.

Dr. William Price was an eccentric man ahead of his time. Dressed in a green coat and trousers, with a red waistcoat and a head-dress of fox skin, he was a familiar figure in the town of Llantrisant where his statue now stands. A pioneer of cremation in Britain, he was arrested and tried in 1884, for cremating the body of his son, to whom he had given the name Iesu Grist (Jesus Christ). He conducted his own defence at his trial in Cardiff, and was acquitted on the payment of one farthing costs. It was this historic judgement that established cremation as a legal practice in Britain.

PENARTH, SOUTH GLAMORGAN
OLD CUSTOM HOUSE

Location: Penarth Marina.

When Penarth's new Docks were opened in 1865, a golden age that would last 100 years lay ahead for South Wales ports. The pleasing classical style of the Custom House, opened in the same year, was a statement of Victorian enterprise and confidence in the future. Over a century and a quarter later, a leisure marina has replaced the docks, and the once proud Custom House, now redundant, stands forlorn and neglected. Clearly in need of a friend, it is well worth the visitor's attention, and perhaps the attention of someone who can give it a new lease of life!

LAVERNOCK POINT
PENARTH, SOUTH GLAMORGAN
MARCONI MEMORIAL

Location: Take the B4267 Penarth—Barry Road, after 2 miles turn left to Lavernock Point, St. Lawrence Church is on the left.

In 1897, Guglielmo Marconi relayed the first radio messages across water. Impatient with the Italian Government's lack of interest in his work, the young pioneer arrived in England. After successfully demonstrating his wireless overland on Salisbury Plain, he brought his apparatus to South Wales for further experiments. A pair of masts 110 feet high were erected at Lavernock Point and on the island of Flat Holm in the Bristol Channel. On the 18th May 1897, Marconi sent the first short message to his assistant George Kemp on the island, "Are You Ready?". It might have been a message for the world, for it was from these early experiments that the radio communications we enjoy today evolved. A bronze plaque commemorating the historic event is set in the wall of St. Lawrence churchyard at Lavernock.

ST. NICHOLAS, SOUTH GLAMORGAN
PREHISTORIC BURIAL CHAMBERS —
TINKINSWOOD & ST. LYTHANS

Location: Take the A48 from Cardiff, at St. Nicholas village turn left down the road signposted Dyffryn House. Signposted.

The great chambered cromlech of Tinkinswood dates back to around 2500 B.C. It is one of the largest and best preserved tombs of its kind in Britain. During excavations in 1914, the bones of about fifty people were discovered, all thought to be members of the same family. Pottery of a much later date was also found in the tomb, lending weight to the theory that it had been re-opened some centuries earlier.

In a field at St. Lythans about a mile from Tinkinswood, there is another ancient tomb (left) in the form of a cairn some 30 metres long. It is similar though smaller than Tinkinswood, and consists of a huge capstone resting on three uprights.

COWBRIDGE, SOUTH GLAMORGAN
COFFIN STILE, LLANFRYNACH CHURCH

> *Location:* At the western end of the Cowbridge bypass, turn left onto an unsigned narrow lane for about ½ mile.

By the churchyard gate leading into the lane is a most unusual stile made of stone. Known as a coffin stile, it is in fact two stiles which are separated in the middle by a stone block on which coffins were laid to rest while the bearers climbed over the stile to enter the churchyard. This type of stile is rare and is thought to be the only one in Glamorgan.

ST. DONAT'S, SOUTH GLAMORGAN
MILLIONAIRE'S CASTLE

Location: Take the B4265 Llantwit Major to Bridgend road — turn left after 2 miles.
Access: Public admitted on 'Open Days'.

In spite of its long history dating back to the 13th century, the Castle of St. Donat's is synonimous with the name of the American millionaire publisher William Randolph Hearst. In a telegraphed message "Buy St. Donat's Castle," to his London representative, Hearst purchased the place in 1925, for $135,000. He spent a fortune restoring it, and the magnificent 14th century arch-braced collar beam roof in Bradenstoke Hall, brought to the castle from tithe barn of Bradenstoke Priory in Wiltshire, is testimony to his zeal. During the twenties and thirties Hearst brought a string of celebrities and a glittering assortment of Hollywood film stars to his castle. Last of them to use it was Bob Hope in 1951, the year in which Hearst died. The castle was sold in 1960 to become the Atlantic College, to which young people now come from all over the world, and in which the Prince of Wales has a special interest.

(Wales Tourist Board)

NEWTON NOTTAGE, PORTHCAWL, MID GLAMORGAN
PRE-REFORMATION STONE WALL PULPIT

Location: St. John Baptist Church is situated on the A4106 in Newton Nottage.

St. John the Baptist at Newton Nottage has an interesting stone pulpit set in the wall of the nave. It is rare, perhaps even unique, and its origin is pre-reformation. Two angels over the arch hold a chalice. They symbolise the Latin word ECCE The Lintel is carved with five crosses representing the five wounds of the crucified Christ. A vine scroll on the cornice symbolises the words AGNUS DEI — to give us ECCE AGNUS DEI "Behold the Lamb of God." Below is a carving depicting the flagellation of Jesus, bound by his feet, hands tied behind his back and naked except for a loin cloth.

The pulpit is only one of many objects of interest in this beautiful church.

MARGAM, MID GLAMORGAN
MARGAM ABBEY ORANGERY

Location: Margam Park is situated 4 miles east of Port Talbot. Leave the
M4 Motorway at Junction 38 to join the A48 and then follow the
signs.
Access: Margam Abbey and Park are open daily throughout the year.

The orangery at Margam is probably the finest classical buildings in Wales. It was built
in 1786, on the site of Margam House by Thomas Mansel Talbot, to house his collection
of exotic orange, lemon and citrus trees. At 327 feet in length, it is the longest orangery
in Britain. Nelson came here in 1802 when touring South Wales with Sir William and
Lady Hamilton. The gardener insisted on charging the distinguished visitors to enter
the park, and then proceeded to show them round. During the last war, the Orangery
was used to accommodate British and American troops. It was completely restored
following the acquisition of Margam Park by Glamorgan County Council in 1973, and
now makes a fine venue for concerts, conferences and other public functions.

*Close by, off the A4211 in Margam, notice the Beulah Octagonal Chapel built in 1838. It used to
stand on the A48. It was carefully removed and rebuilt on its present site, to make way for the M4
Motorway.*

PORT TALBOT, MID GLAMORGAN
GRAVE OF DIC PENDERYN.

Location: St. Mary's Churchyard, Port Talbot.

In June, 1831, Merthyr Tydfil was the scene of violent riots in which troops were deployed and shots were fired. Richard Lewis, a miner known locally as Dic Penderyn, was arrested with others and accused of felinously attacking and wounding a soldier. The men were tried and sentenced to transportation; except Lewis who was sentenced to death. Pleas for clemency were rejected, and on the 13th August 1831, he was publicly hanged in Cardiff. From the gallows he declared: "I am going to suffer unjustly. God who knows all things knows it is so." Minutes later he was dead. Escorted by a large crowd, his body was taken on a cart to Port Talbot, where he was buried in St. Mary's churchyard where his grave is marked by a granite cross.

ABERCRAVE, SWANSEA VALLEY, POWYS
CASTLE HOME OF THE QUEEN OF SONG

Location: Two miles north of Abercrave on the A4067.
Access: Craig-y-Nos is now an arts centre and hotel with an excellent restaurant and a bar, which are open to the public.

The industrial Swansea Valley is perhaps an unlikely place to find the home of one of the greatest operatic stars of all time. Yet it was here in the remote upper reaches of the valley that the Victorian Queen of Song, Adelina Patti made her home. From here she travelled the world, sang in its greatest opera houses and was received like royalty.

Craig-y-Nos was her retreat from the world; a place to relax and entertain her friends, who included composers, musicians, artists and nobility and royalty. The Castle has a magnificent ornate bijou theatre which was modelled on Drury Lane, and built so she could sing for her guests. It has been remarkably preserved and is still in regular use. The Castle was Patti's home for forty years, until her death there in 1919.

Stage, Bijou Theatre

Bijou Theatre

SWANSEA, WEST GLAMORGAN
BRITISH EMPIRE PANELS

> *Location:* Brangwyn Hall, Guildhall, Swansea.
> *Access:* The Guildhall is open to the public during normal office hours on weekdays.

In 1924, the House of Lords decided to commemorate the First World War with a set of murals to decorate the Royal Gallery in the Palace of Westminster. The artist Frank Brangwyn was commissioned to execute the work, but instead of depicting the horrors of war, he filled the large spaces with colourful scenes of life in the British Empire. By 1930 most of the commission was complete and displayed to the Noble Lords, who rejected the work. The murals, consisting of seventeen large panels, the largest measuring 20 x 15 feet were purchased in 1934 by Swansea Corporation for the new Guildhall. Visitors will surely agree that the House of Lord's loss was Swansea's gain. The assembly hall in which the murals are displayed was named Brangwyn Hall in honour of the artist.

Section of British Empire Panel

OYSTERMOUTH, SWANSEA, WEST GLAMORGAN
MUMBLES RAILWAY WINDOWS

Location: Oystermouth Parish Church, Mumbles.

Three stained glass windows in Oystermouth Church commemorate the evolution of what was known as The Mumbles Railway. It is claimed to have been the first and oldest passenger railway in the world, though strictly speaking it was not a railway, but a tramway. It started with horsedrawn trams before the Napoleonic wars, running along the levelled sandhills between Swansea in the east to Oystermouth in the west. Later it entered the age of steam, and in 1929 converted to electricity. Its long history ended on 5th January 1960, when a large crowd witnessed the departure of the last tram from Rutland Street Depot. The windows in Oystermouth Church are an affectionate reminder of a much loved form of transport.

OYSTERMOUTH, SWANSEA, WEST GLAMORGAN
BOWDLER'S GRAVE

> *Location:* Oystermouth Churchyard.

Look up the word 'bowdlerize' in the Oxford Dictionary and it will tell you it means, 'to expurgate'. But where did the word originate? The answer lies beneath a simple tombstone in Oystermouth churchyard. It marks the grave of Thomas Bowdler, a doctor of medicine, and Chairman of the Society for the Suppression of Vice, who went to live at Oystermouth in 1810. A virtuous man, for much of his life, he waged a crusade against bawdy literature. His targets included the works of Shakespeare and even the Bible. In 1818 he published 'The Family Shakespeare' with all the naughty words erased. He went on to edit the Bible into respectable family reading, and was well on the way to cleaning up Gibbon's *Rise and Fall of the Roman Empire* at the time of his death in 1825. One wonders what he would make of today's tabloid press.

OYSTERMOUTH, SWANSEA, WEST GLAMORGAN
SANTIAGO BELLS

Location: Oystermouth Parish Church.

Three interesting bells stand silent in the porch of Oystermouth Parish Church. These are no ordinary bells, having been brought here with several others from Chile. They came from the Cathedral Church of la Campaniel in Santiago, which was destroyed by a fire in 1863, in which 2000 worshipers died. Three other bells were hung in the church tower at Oystermouth. The bells bear Latin and Spanish inscriptions.

MUMBLES
MUMBLES LIGHTHOUSE

> *Location:* Situated on the outer of two islets at the western end of Swansea Bay.
> *Access:* Not open to the public.

Swansea Town Council received permission to build a lighthouse and keeper's dwellings on Mumbles Head in 1794, its function to guide shipping safely into Swansea Bay past the Mumbles, a small group of rocks.

Initially the light was provided by two coal fires, one fire set several feet above the other on a stone tower. This was later replaced by Argand lamps and reflectors.

The present lighthouse consists of a 56ft-high tower, the light 114 feet above mean water level, and with a range of 19 miles. When operational the diaphone fog signal gives three blasts every 60 seconds.

Other lighthouses of interest in South Wales include: Strumble Head (nr. Fishguard); St Ann's Head (nr. Milford Haven); Caldy Island (nr. Tenby); Nash Point (nr. Llantwit Major); and East Usk (nr. Newport).

PENRICE, GOWER, WEST GLAMORGAN
PIGEON COTE AND GRANARY

Location: Home Farm, Penrice, A4118 from Swansea.

Brick built and standing on straddle stones in a private garden, this unusual pigeon cote and granary is easily viewed from the road.

PORT EYNON, GOWER, WEST GLAMORGAN
MEMORIAL TO LIFEBOATMEN

Location: St. Cattwg's Churchyard.

Gravestones in Gower's churchyards are a sad reminder of man's constant battle with the sea. Perhaps the most moving memorial is the Lifeboatman at Port Eynon, erected in the churchyard following the loss of three men from the local lifeboat "Janet" in 1916.

The boat put to sea on New Year's Day to help the S.S. *Dunvegan,* but only a pilot was needed. Making for home in a howling gale the lifeboat turned over and two men were lost. Miraculously, the crew managed to right her, and had almost regained control when the boat was hit by another huge wave. All the men were thrown into the sea, and another was lost. The survivors regained control and in darkness rowed for Mumbles. They came ashore at nine'o clock on the following morning after more than twenty hours at sea. Coxswain Billy Gibbs, Second Coxswain William Eynon, and Lifeboatman George Harry were tragically lost.

RHOSSILI, GOWER, WEST GLAMORGAN
MEMORIAL TO AN ANTARCTIC HERO

Location: Parish Church.

A simple plaque on the wall of Rhossili Church commemorates a local man, Petty Officer Edgar Evans R.N., the Equipment Officer who died during Scott's ill-fated expedition to the South Pole. A celebrating man, he sometimes became, as they say, a little bit legless. This happened at a reception in Cardiff, where he overindulged the Lord Mayor's hospitality, and had to be carried back to the boat. Worse was to befall him in New Zealand where he fell into the harbour after over imbibing, and was nearly dismissed. But in spite of his shortcomings, he was highly regarded by Scott, with whom he reached the South Pole on 17th January 1912. Sadly they all perished. *Terra Nova's* log recorded: "... all lost on the return journey dying from exposure and want." Evans would have had much to celebrate had he made it back to his home in Rhossili.

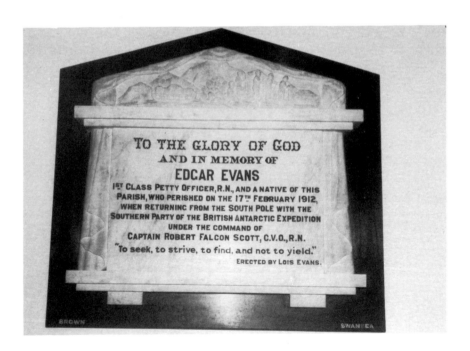

BUILTH WELLS
MEMORIAL TO PRINCE LLYWELYN

Location: By the roadside at Climery, 4 miles west of Builth.

(Wales Tourist Board)

Llywelin ap Iorwerth was slain near Builth Wells in December 1282. He was the first and the last native ruler to be acknowledged as Prince of Wales by the English. His head was severed and displayed over a gate in the Tower of London. Today a simple stone with an English inscription commemorates the place near where he was slain.

LLANDOVERY, DYFED
MAILCOACH MEMORIAL

Location: 2 miles east of Llandovery on the A40 Brecon road on the right.

On the A40 road two miles east of Llandovery, is an interesting reminder of the hazards of old coaching days. A grey stone pillar records how on the 19th December 1835, the Gloucester to Carmarthen Coach carrying passengers and mail, plunged over a precipice. The inscription records that the driver, Edward Jenkins, was intoxicated. Driving his horses hard at full speed on the wrong side of the road, he met a cart coming from the opposite direction. For the two lead horses, there seemed only one way to go. Leaping a fence they took coach and passengers with them, rolling over and over for 121 feet down the steep bank towards the river below.

Providence intervened in the form of an ash tree against which coach and horses came to rest. One of the passengers landed in the river, but no one was killed. A Colonel Gwynn, who was travelling on top of the coach was so incensed, that he administered summary justice by giving the driver a good kick in the posterior.

LLANARTHNEY, DYFED
PAXTON'S TOWER

> *Location:* 6 miles east of Carmarthen off the B4300.
> *Access:* Owned by National Trust and open to the public.

Paxton's Tower, stands on a lush hillside above the River Tawe. It is a fine stone triangular folly, built by the wealthy Sir William Paxton who dedicated it to Nelson soon after Trafalgar. Above each of the three entrances is an inscription in English, Welsh and Latin. the English version reads:

"To the Invincible Commander Viscount Nelson in Commemoration of Deeds before the Walls of Copenhagen, and on the shores of Spain; of the Empire everywhere maintained by him over the seas; and of the death which in the fulness of his own glory, though ultimately for his own Country and for Europe, conquring he died. This Tower was erected by William Paxton."

The tower commands extensive views of seven counties, and Paxton reckoned that from the top of the tower on a clear day, he could with the aid of field glasses, see his carriage with two pairs of white horses being driven out of Tenby, 30 miles distant.

(Wales Tourist Board)

67

LAUGHARNE, PEMBROKESHIRE
DYLAN THOMAS' BOAT HOUSE

Location: Laugharne is on the A4066, 14 miles south west of Carmarthen.
Access: Along a narrow cliff path, named Dylan's Walk.

"This timeless, mild beguiling island of a town," was one of Dylan Thomas's many descriptions of Laugharne, where in 1949 he returned to live after years of absence. He arrived in spring with a pregnant wife, and made his home in the Boat House along an overgrown cliff path, now known as Dylan's Walk. The house commands magnificent views across ". . . the flat sad estuary sands." Here in the draught and damp of an ivy-covered rough wooden hut, set apart from the house and standing on stilts, he wrote some of his most memorable works. This pleasing little West Wales town was featured in his Play for Voices, 'Under Milk Wood', thinly disguised as the romantically eccentric Llareggub. Now a museum and place of pilgrimage for visitors from all over the world, the Boat House is open to the public.

(Wales Tourist Board).

68

LAUGHARNE, PEMBROKESHIRE
DYLAN THOMAS' GRAVE

Location: Churchyard, Laugharne.

When Dylan Thomas died in 1953, on a reading tour of America, his body was brought home to be buried at Laugharne. He lies in a simple grave in the churchyard, marked by a white wooden cross. According to his biographers, the poet lived a turbulent life at Laugharne before and after the last war; first in a fisherman's cottage on Gosport Street, before moving to . . . "a tall and dignified house at the posh end of town," . . . Latterly he lived in what is now the Boat House shrine.

(Wales Tourist Board)

69

CAREW, PEMBROKESHIRE
CAREW CASTLE

> *Location:* The village of Carew is on the A4075, 4 miles north-east of Pembroke
> *Access:* Open to the public daily.

Carew Castle stands majestically on the banks of the River Cleddau. Though only a shell, its charming windows still give it a lived in appearance. The castle was owned by Sir Rhys ap Thomas, a friend of Henry Tudor, later to be Henry VII. It is said that he stayed at the castle in 1485, on his way from Milford to Bosworth. Sir Rhys ap Thomas was renowned for his extravagant hospitality, and is remembered for a celebration of St. George's Day that lasted a week. On the banks of the river near to the Castle is a 'French Tidal Mill' dating back to 1560, which is open to visitors as a working museum.

(Wales Tourist Board)

CAREW, PEMBROKESHIRE
CELTIC CROSS

Location: The village of Carew is on the A4075 4 miles north-east of Pembroke.

The Carew Cross must surely be one of the finest examples of Celtic craftmanship in existence. The tall wheel headed cross, thought to be of the 11th century, is sited near to the Castle on the A4075 road that runs through Carew village. It is the largest and best preserved cross of a group of composite crosses, another fine example being the one at Nevern. The inscription on the cross reads: Margiteut, rex Etg, (uin) filius — meaning King Margiteut son of Etguin Maredudd ap Edwin. He was joint ruler of the Kingdon Of Dehueubarth (ie south west Wales), from 1033 until his death in 1035. The cross is thought to commemorate his gift of land to the Church.

(Wales Tourist Board)

FISHGUARD, PEMBROKESHIRE
LAST INVASION OF BRITAIN

Location: Town Square.

The Pembrokeshire town of Fishguard has a unique place in British history, being the scene of the last invasion of Britain by foreign troops. On the 22nd February 1797, 600 French soldiers and 800 ex-convicts, lead by an Irish-American General called William Tate, landed near Carreg Wastad Point, north of Fishguard. They were met by the local militia known as the Fishguard Fencibles lead by Lord Cawdor, who rounded them up. But it is said that the sight of a large crowd of Welsh women wearing traditional red shawls and tall black hats was what really convinced the French the odds were against them, Heroine of the hour was Jemima Nicholas who, armed with a pitchfork, captured several invaders single handed. She is commemorated in St. Mary's churchyard by a stone that records her heroic act. Almost next door to the church is the Royal Oak Inn, where Tate signed the surrender of his troops on a table still to be seen inside. A tablet above the door of the inn records the historic event (see back cover).

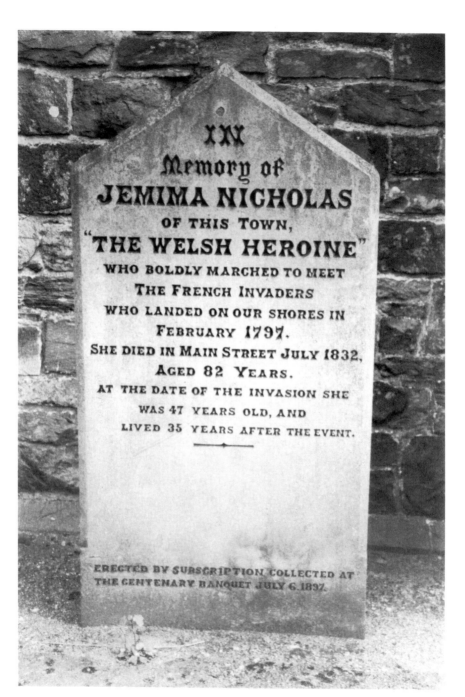

In
Memory of
JEMIMA NICHOLAS
OF THIS TOWN,
"THE WELSH HEROINE"
WHO BOLDLY MARCHED TO MEET
THE FRENCH INVADERS
WHO LANDED ON OUR SHORES IN
FEBRUARY 1797.
SHE DIED IN MAIN STREET JULY 1832,
AGED 82 YEARS.
AT THE DATE OF THE INVASION SHE
WAS 47 YEARS OLD, AND
LIVED 35 YEARS AFTER THE EVENT.

ERECTED BY SUBSCRIPTION COLLECTED AT
THE CENTENARY BANQUET JULY 6 1897.

CWM-YR-EGLWYS, DINAS, PEMROKESHIRE
ST. BRYNACH'S CHAPEL

Location: Take the A487, situated 4 miles north-east of Fishguard through Dinas Cross, then left down the narrow road signposted to Cwm-yr-Eglwys, for about one mile.

Cwm-yr-Eglwys is a little known inlet on the Pembrokeshire coast. The views across Newport Bay are quite stunning, particularly on a clear summer evening when the sun is setting. It is a haven of peace, made more tranquil by the remains of St. Brynach's 12th century Celtic style church. Now only the belfry and part of the west wall remain, with a few simple gravestones written in English and Welsh. The church was destroyed in the great storm of October 1859, which claimed 113 ships off the coast of Wales. In March 1979, severe storms caused further extensive damage to the churchyard, which has since been restored by Presely District Council.

NEVERN, PEMBROKESHIRE
CELTIC CROSS

Location: Church Yard, St Brynach's Church.

St. Brynach's Cross at Nevern, is a perfect example of Celtic craftmanship. Carved from Preseli 'blue stone', it stands among the churchyard yews, in a state of preservation that belies its antiquity. Legend says that a broken branch of one of the yews, bleads in mourning for the last Welsh Prince of Wales, and will not cease until there is another. The cuckoo was St. Brynach's bird, and according to local legend, the first cuckoo of spring sings from the cross on his feast day, the 7th April.

(Wales Tourist Board)

75

NEVERN, PEMBROKESHIRE
PENTRE IFAN CROMLECH

> *Location:* Two miles south-east of Nevern, 3½ miles south-east of Newport off the A487.

Since time immemorial, man has used the 'blue stone' of the Preseli Hills for religious purposes. The huge stones at Stonehenge on Salisbury Plain were miraculously transported from here for almost 200 miles over land and water. In the northern foothills a few miles from Newport, is Pentre Ifan Cromlech, an ancient burial chamber consisting of three upright stones supporting a gigantic 16 ft capstone, hewn from the hills of Preseli.

(Wales Tourist Board)

ST. DAVID' PEMBROKESHIRE
ST. NON'S CHAPEL AND HOLY WELL

Location: Above St. Non's Bay.

Take the road for Porth Clais from St. David's for about a mile towards St. Non's Bay. Signposted across the field from the car park are the ruins of St. Non's Chapel, which according to tradition, marks the site of St. David's birth. Nearby is the holy well, dedicated to St. Non, the mother of St. David. The spring is said to have appeared on the night St. David was born.

St. Non, the mother of St. David

ST. DAVID'S, PEMBROKESHIRE
RELIC OF A SAINT

Location: St. David's Cathedral.

Set in a reliquery behind the High Altar of St. David's Cathedral is a casket containing the mortal remains of Wales' Patron Saint. St. David's was an important place of pilgrimage for early Christians. Two visits to the tomb of the Saint were regarded as being equal to one pilgrimage to Rome, and three equal to a visit to Jerusalem's Holy Sepulchre. Though perhaps of lesser importance today, St. David's is still a much loved place of pilgrimage.

MILFORD HAVEN, PEMBROKESHIRE
NELSON HOTEL

Location: Hamilton Terrace.

In August 1802, Nelson paid a visit to Milford Haven with his friends Sir William and Lady Hamilton. They stayed at the New Inn, which had been opened two years earlier. It was subsequently renamed the Lord Nelson Hotel, to commemorate the visit. The hotel was the scene of a sumptuous banquet in Nelson's honour, attended by all the nobility and gentry of Pembrokeshire. Nelson presented the hotel with a portrait of himself, painted by the well known artist Guzzardi at Palermo. It now hangs in the Admiralty in London.

PEMBROKE DOCK, PEMBROKESHIRE
EARLY POSTAL VENDING MACHINE

Location: Pembroke Street, Pembroke Dock.

A charming Victorian curiosity is to be found behind a piece of protective glass in the wall of Pembroke Dock Market. It is an early vending machine which dispensed penny postage stamps complete with paper and envelopes. It also dispensed postcards with halfpenny stamps.

PEMBROKE
PEMBROKE CASTLE

For centuries Pembroke Castle has dominated this historic town, which the Welsh Chieftain Rhys ap Tudur held against the Norman onslaught. The castle we see today dates from the late 12th century, and is the work of Richard Strongbow's son in law, William Marshall. It was he who built the Great Round Keep with walls that are 20ft thick. Energetic visitors prepared to climb the steps to the top of the keep will be rewarded with a breathtaking view of the castle and town. It was here that Harri Tudur, the Welshman who became King Henry VII was born in 1456. His birthplace was a room on the first floor of the tower that now bears his name. Henry remained in Pembroke until 1471, when a Welsh revolt compelled him to flee to Brittany. For six years during the Civil War, Pembroke was held for Cromwell, until the Mayor defected to the cause of the King. Pembroke was so important to Parliament, that Cromwell himself conducted the siege. The Mayor was taken to London and shot by a firing squad, and the castle reduced to a ruin.

(Wales Tourist Board)

ANGLE, PEMBROKESHIRE
FISHERMEN'S CHAPEL, DOVECOTE AND PELE TOWER

Location: Parish Churchyard.

Angle has a curious collection of historic buildings in and around the churchyard. To the side of the church is the tiny 'Fisherman's Chapel', dedicated to St. Anthony, founded by Edward de Shirburn of Nangle, and built in 1447. Separated from the chapel at high tide is a moated enclosure with a pele tower, and in a field nearby is an interesting stone circular dovecote.

Dovecote, Angle

BOSHERTON, PEMBROKESHIRE
ST. GOVAN'S CHAPEL

Location: Through the village of Bosherton, the chapel is signposted off the B4319 Castlemartin — Stackpole Road. Army Firing Range — Danger Zone.

Access: No Access when the warning flag is flying.

The tiny stone chapel of St. Govan is wedged in the rugged rocks of the Pembrokeshire coast. Steeped in myth and legend, it must be one of the county's most intriguing curiosities. A holy hermit, reputed to have been Sir Gawain of Arthurian legend, is said to have occupied a cell on the site. The chapel has a simple stone altar and stone seating along its walls. Set in a wall to the side of the doorway is a holy water stoup. The chapel has three windows and a doorway that leads out to the rocks and the sea. Access is by seventy steep steps that can be hazardous in wet weather, and not recommended to the old or infirm.

TENBY, PEMBROKESHIRE
TUDOR MERCHANT'S HOUSE

Location: Quay Hill, Tenby.
Access: The house is owned by the National Trust, and open to the public from 30th March to 31st October.

The Tudor Merchant's House is an important part of Tenby's heritage, and a fine example of medieval architecture that reflects the prosperity of the town and its merchants. Built in the late 15th century, its construction is typical of its period in south west Wales. There are remains of early frescos incorporating a floral pattern on three interior walls.

TENBY, PEMBROKESHIRE
MEMORIAL TO A MATHEMATICAL GENIUS

> *Location:* Tenby Parish Church.

Robert Recorde was the brilliant Elizabethan mathematician. School children might be interested to know that he was the first man to work out square roots, and the man who invented the equals (=) sign. He was also the Court Physician to Edward VI and Mary I. His memorial is a plaque on a wall inside the church.

CADAVER TOMB OF THOMAS DANBY

In an arched recess in the north aisle of Tenby Church is the tomb of Thomas Danby who died circa 1499. He was the Tenby priest who risked his life hiding and aiding the escape of the future King Henry VII, and his uncle Jasper Tudor, Earl of Pembroke, after the Battle of Tewkesbury. Here, Danby is portrayed, not in his ecclesiastical finery, but as a semi-naked decomposing corpse. The chilling message is clear to all: "As I am now, so shall ye be." a sober reminder of our mortality.

(Roger Worsley)

TENBY, PEMBROKESHIRE
GOTHIC LIME KILNS

> *Location:* Lime Kiln Caravan Park, 1 mile south-west of Tenby on the
> A4139 Penally road.
> *Access:* Non-resident visitors are allowed to inspect the Kilns.

For centuries, lime making prospered as an important industry in Wales, the earliest
known kilns dating back to 1325. Limekilns can be found all over the Principality; there
are more than two hundred and fifty in Pembrokeshire alone. But the industry started
to decline when the railways arrived in the middle of last century, when it became
cheaper to import lime from elsewhere. The decline however, was slow, with kilns
surviving in Solva and Haverfordwest well into the 1930s. Some of the kilns were
works of real architectural merit, the ones at Mynydd y Garreg above Kidwelly, have
been described as reminiscent of the Valley of the Kings. At Tenby, the Gothic style
kilns were designed by the celebrated John Nash, creator of such architectural gems as
the Pavilion at Brighton, London's Regent Street, and the nash Terraces in Regent's
Park. Few mourned the passing of lime making which was a hard and dangerous
occupation. Workers lived at the kilns in limeburners' huts, which were situated
upwind of the lethal gasses. Vagrants seeking a warm place for the night on top of the
kilns, were often overcome by gas and fell into the red hot workings, to be burnt
beyond recognition.

(Roger Worsley)